Contents

Competitive Doubles

Types of takeout doubles are the most common doubles used in competitive situations and account for the majority of all doubles. They are simply doubles designed to show a desire for partner to bid one of the suits not yet bid. The point range varies depending on:

- Position you are in – opener, responder, overcaller, or responder to overcaller (sometimes called Advancer); and
- Level at which partner's response is forced to be made.

The suits the double shows depend on how the auction has proceeded.

There are two additional doubles, Maximal Doubles and Support Doubles, used to indicate raises in competitive auctions that you will find equally useful.

A brief description of each of these competitive doubles and which player might bid the double is provided in the following table.

Name of Double	Position	Description
Takeout	Overcaller	Opening hand, shortness in opener's suit and at least three cards in the remaining three suits (if two suits have been bid, double shows at least four cards in the remaining two suits).
Negative	Responder	6+ points, shows the two unbid suits or if only one major has been bid, it shows 4+ cards in the other major.
Responsive	Advancer	6+ points, shows the two unbid suits, 4+/4+.
Snapdragon	Advancer	6+ points, after three suits have been bid it shows the unbid suit 5+ cards and usually a tolerance (2+ cards) for the suit partner bid.
Balancing	Overcaller	Doubling when the auction has ended at a low level showing shortness (0-1-2) in the opponents' suits.
Re-opening	Any position but most often associated with the opening bidder.	In any auction, this bid shows a hand that desires for the auction to continue but has no clear bid. Generally it is expected that partner will bid but they may pass for penalty.
Support	Opener	In a competitive auction when opener's right hand opponent overcalled a suit below the two-level of responder's suit.
Maximal	Opener (occasionally Advancer)	In a competitive auction when opener's right hand opponent bid the suit, at the three level, directly in rank below the major suit opener and responder have bid and raised.

In the following pages let's look in detail at the requirements for each of these doubles and how partner will respond.

Takeout Doubles

Takeout Doubles

A Takeout Double is a double made by an overcaller. An opponent opens the bidding and overcaller says the word "double". This bid shows:

- Shortness (0-1-2) in the suit opened;
- 11+ points (unless partner is doubling a pre-emptive bid. In that case, the double should show a better hand in either high card points or distribution to compensate for forcing partner to respond at the three or four level); and
- At least three cards in each of the remaining three suits.

Note: If two suits have been bid, double promises four cards in each of the remaining two suits and does not promise specific shortness in any other suit.

If your partner doubles and your right hand opponent (RHO) passes, you must bid. If your RHO bids, you may still bid, but are not required to bid.

Generally, partner to the doubler will bid his longest suit. His high card points (HCPs) determine the level at which he will bid. With:

- 0 to 9 points bid at the cheapest level;

- 9+ to 12 points skip one level; or
- 12+ points consider game somewhere.

One exception is that after your partner has made a Takeout double of a minor suit and partner of the doubler has *10+ points and at least four cards in both majors*; he may cuebid (bid opener's suit) and ask the doubler to bid his longest major. With equal length in the majors and 11-15 points, the doubler would bid hearts.

Occasionally, if your choice is between a major or a minor suit, you might choose to bid your major suit (even if it is shorter) because of the advantage in either scoring or being able to bid at a lower level. An example:

North	East	South	West
1♥	DBL	Pass	?

Since South passed, regardless of his points, West must bid. West holds:

♠Q765 ♥73 ♦A8543 ♣54

West has longer diamonds, but he can bid spades at the one level and if he is successful in his contract, he will get more points for playing spades than diamonds. West will bid 1♠.

Responder should never choose to bid the suit the opponents have opened. *Remember, the doubler has shortness in the suit the opponent opened. Doubler will not have support in the opponents' suit.*

Very seldom is it right to play No Trump after a Takeout Double has been bid, especially if the opening bid was one of a major suit since you know the opponents will have a long suit they can lead to establish tricks. Only consider NT when you have:

- A stopper (a high card in the opponents' suit);
- No long suit that you would like to bid; and
- Constructive values (8+ HCP).

After his partner bids, doubler will have another opportunity to bid. The doubler should always keep in mind what his first bid (double) told his partner about his hand and what responder's bid indicated to him.

Doubler needs to consider:

- How many points does responder have?;
- How many cards in the suit did responder promise?; and
- Have the opponent's bid again?

All of these factors will come into play when the doubler is deciding whether to pass or bid at his next opportunity. In general, unless responder has promised some values and/or length in his suit, doubler will pass at his next opportunity to bid.

The only exceptions where the doubler would bid with minimum values, would be in the following types of auction:

North	East	South	West
1♣	Dbl	1♠	2♥
2♠	?		

West did not have to bid, but chose to. West should have some values (6-8 pts). If East passes 2♠, West will be unsure whether East has four hearts or only three. Therefore, with four hearts East should bid again. This would not show extra values.

North	East	South	West
1♣	Dbl	Pass	1♥
2♣	?		

West did not jump, did not show any extra values, nor did he show any specific amount of hearts (though we expect he has four). However, if East passes, the opponents may play in 2♣. East may bid 2♥ with four hearts and a solid (12+ points) take out double. This bid would not invite game.

North	East	South	West
1♣	Dbl	Pass	1♥
Pass	?		

West was forced to bid, since South passed. East/West have the contract at this point. If East raises in this situation it is a "free" raise. He does not have to bid in order for he and partner to play the hand, but would be choosing to bid anyway, that is a free raise. Raising hearts in this auction, shows that East has four hearts and invites his partner to bid game with 6-8 points (since he knows that partner has less than 9 points based on his failure to jump to 2♥).

The difference in these auctions is what both East and West had promised with their initial bids and the action(s) taken by the opponents.

One last comment about Takeout doubles must be made. It is the exception to the rules governing a Takeout Double. This occurs when overcaller has 18+ points (or the equivalent in length and/or high-cards) and wants to tell his partner that his hand is much better than advancer would expect if they simply overcalled.

With this type of hand, overcaller doubles and then bids a suit (or NT) of his own. This "sounds" like a Takeout Double but his subsequent bid identifies the double as a "value showing double". It is not until overcaller's second bid that advancer realizes the difference.

The auction would proceed:

North	East	South	West
1♣	Dbl	Pass	1♥
Pass	?		

If East, after doubling at his first opportunity to bid, chooses to bid a new suit or NT, he is showing 18+ points and inviting game. If West (advancer) has "a trick and a fit", he should raise East to game. A trick is an ace, a king or, if you have a fit for East's suit, a singleton or void in another suit. A fit is 3+ cards or A, K or Q and one or more cards in East's suit. If East had the suit responder bid (hearts) he would bid 3♥ or 4♥ depending on how many tricks he thinks he can take, knowing that partner has four hearts.

Takeout Double

Board 1
North Deals
None Vul

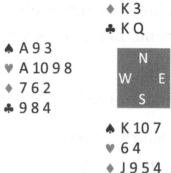

♠ Q J 8 6 4 2
♥ J 5 3
♦ K 3
♣ K Q

♠ A 9 3
♥ A 10 9 8
♦ 7 6 2
♣ 9 8 4

♠ 5
♥ K Q 7 2
♦ A Q 10 8
♣ A J 7 3

♠ K 10 7
♥ 6 4
♦ J 9 5 4
♣ 10 6 5 2

West	North	East	South
	1 ♠	Dbl	Pass
2 ♥	Pass	3 ♥	Pass
4 ♥	Pass	Pass	Pass

East's Double is a Takeout Double showing shortness in spades, 11+ points and at least three cards in the remaining three suits.

Since South passed, West must bid and chooses hearts.

With a hand that evaluates to 18 points in support of hearts, East freely raises hearts suggesting to East that they might play game in hearts.

With 8 points, West accepts the invitation to game and bids 4♥.

Takeout Double

Board 2
East Deals
N-S Vul

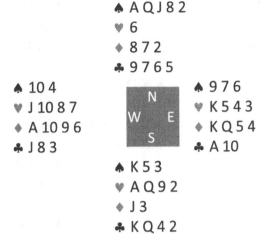

```
              ♠ A Q J 8 2
              ♥ 6
              ♦ 8 7 2
              ♣ 9 7 6 5

  ♠ 10 4                    ♠ 9 7 6
  ♥ J 10 8 7        N       ♥ K 5 4 3
  ♦ A 10 9 6    W       E   ♦ K Q 5 4
  ♣ J 8 3           S       ♣ A 10

              ♠ K 5 3
              ♥ A Q 9 2
              ♦ J 3
              ♣ K Q 4 2
```

West	North	East	South
		1 ♦	Dbl
1 ♥	1 ♠	2 ♥	Pass
Pass	2 ♠	Pass	Pass
Pass			

South's Double is a Takeout Double showing shortness in diamonds, 11+ points and at least three cards in every other suit.

North freely bids 1♠ which shows at least six points, but no more than nine points.

South has only three spades, so passes 2♥. North can easily bid 2♠ since he has already limited his hand to less than 9 points. He does not promise extra values when he bids a second time.

Takeout Double

Board 3
South Deals
E-W Vul

♠ 10 8
♥ 9 7 3
♦ A 10 6 4 2
♣ 8 7 3

♠ K Q 6 2
♥ 10
♦ Q 9 7 5 3
♣ A Q 2

```
    N
W       E
    S
```

♠ J 9 7 5
♥ K 5 4
♦ K 8
♣ K 10 6 4

♠ A 4 3
♥ A Q J 8 6 2
♦ J
♣ J 9 5

West	North	East	South
			1 ♥
Dbl	Pass	2 ♠	Pass
4 ♠	Pass	Pass	Pass

West does not overcall since his five-card suit is not very strong. Instead, West doubles showing shortness in hearts, 11+ points and at least three cards in the remaining three suits.

East jumps to 2♠, showing 9+ to 11 points and at least four spades.

West bids game in spades with four spades, a singleton, a side five-card suit and a hand that evaluates to 15 points in support of spades.

Takeout Double

Board 4
West Deals
Both Vul

	♠ K Q 4 2	
	♥ J 9 2	
	♦ 9 7	
	♣ A 9 5 4	

♠ 10 5		♠ 9 6 3
♥ 10 7 3	N	♥ K 6 4
♦ Q J 10 6 3	W E	♦ A K 5 2
♣ 8 6 2	S	♣ Q J 3

	♠ A J 8 7	
	♥ A Q 8 5	
	♦ 8 4	
	♣ K 10 7	

West	North	East	South
Pass	Pass	1 ♦	Dbl
Pass	2 ♠	Pass	3 ♠
Pass	Pass	Pass	

South's double is a Takeout Double showing shortness in diamonds, 11+ points and at least three cards in the remaining three suits.

North's skip bid to 2♠, shows 9+ to 11 points.

South bids 3♠ confirming an eight card fit with a slightly better hand than he has to have for his double and North passes with minimum values for his jump.

Negative Doubles

Negative Doubles

A Negative Double is a double made by responder to opener. This double occurs after opener opens the bidding with one of a suit and their left hand opponent overcalls a suit. Responder promises enough points (6+ HCPs) to have responded to the opening bidder. Traditionally, a Negative Double promised at least four cards in the remaining two unbid suits, not the suit partner opened and not the suit overcaller bid.

In modern bridge we've changed this just a little due to our infatuation with finding a major suit fit. Here are the modern rules:

If two major suits have been bid, double promises both minor suits, at least four cards in each. An example:

North	East	South	West
1♥	1♠	?	

South holds:

♠765 ♥73 ♦A743 ♣Q542

South would say the word "double". Since South is responder, this double must be a Negative Double showing 4+ diamonds, 4+ clubs and 6+ points.

If two minor suits have been bid, double promises both major suits, at least four cards in each. An example:

North	East	South	West
1♦	2♣	?	

South holds:

♠Q765 ♥A973 ♦K3 ♣A52

South would say the word "double". Since South is responder, this double must be a Negative Double showing 4+ spades, 4+ hearts and 6+ points

Here is our change in modern bidding methods: *if one major has been bid, double promises at least four cards in the unbid major.*

North	East	South	West
1♥	2♣	?	

South holds:

♠Q765 ♥73 ♦A43 ♣8542

South would say the word "double". Since South is responder, this double must be a Negative Double showing 4+ spades and 6+ points.

Note that South would also say double if his hand were:

♠Q7654   ♥73   ♦A43   ♣852

Since bidding a new suit at the two level would have promised **10+ points** (South only has 6 points), and a 5+ card suit, double is the only bid that allows South to tell his partner that he has a spade suit.

Note that South would also double if his hand were:

♠Q764   ♥73   ♦AKJ3   ♣852

Since bidding a new suit at the two level would have promised 10+ points and a **5+ card suit** (South only has four spades), double is the only bid that allows South to tell his partner that he has a spade suit.

Another example:

North	East	South	West
1♣	1♠	?	

South would say the word "double". Since South is responder, this double must be a Negative Double showing 4+ hearts and 6+ points

In all examples opener rebids as he would have without the opponent's overcall. With:

- A fit for responder's suit and a minimum (12-15 pts.) hand, he bids the suit at the minimum level;
- A fit for responder's suit and a medium (15+ to 18- pts.) hand, he bids the suit skipping one level;
- A fit for responder's major suit and a maximum (18+ pts.) hand, he bids the suit at the game level; and
- Without a fit, he bids as he would have had responder bid a new suit at the one level.

Negative Doubles occur very often and will be invaluable to your success.

Negative Double

Board 5
North Deals
N-S Vul

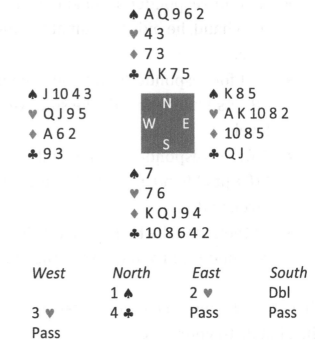

♠ A Q 9 6 2
♥ 4 3
♦ 7 3
♣ A K 7 5

♠ J 10 4 3
♥ Q J 9 5
♦ A 6 2
♣ 9 3

♠ K 8 5
♥ A K 10 8 2
♦ 10 8 5
♣ Q J

♠ 7
♥ 7 6
♦ K Q J 9 4
♣ 10 8 6 4 2

West	North	East	South
	1 ♠	2 ♥	Dbl
3 ♥	4 ♣	Pass	Pass
Pass			

South's double is a Negative Double. Since two majors have been bid, South's double shows both minors. South promises at least four cards in both suits and at least 6 points.

Since South is forcing North to bid at the three level, South should have more points or more shape (more cards in his suits) or both.

Negative Double

Board 6
East Deals
E-W Vul

```
              ♠ 9 8 2
              ♥ K 6 4
              ♦ 8 7 2
              ♣ K 7 6 3
♠ A J 10 4              ♠ K Q 7 6
♥ J 8 7        N        ♥ 10 5
♦ J 10 4    W     E     ♦ K Q 6 5
♣ J 10 8       S       ♣ A 9 5
              ♠ 5 3
              ♥ A Q 9 3 2
              ♦ A 9 3
              ♣ Q 4 2
```

West	North	East	South
		1 ♦	1 ♥
Dbl	2 ♥	3 ♠	Pass
Pass	Pass		

West's double is a Negative Double. Since one major has been bid, West is showing exactly four spades and at least six points. *Remember that when you have Negative Double available, bidding 1♠ over 1♥ would promise 5+ spades.*

East has 15 high card points and a singleton. With a hand that evaluates to 17 points in support of spades, East bids 3♠. With a minimum, West passes.

Negative Double

Board 7
South Deals
Both Vul

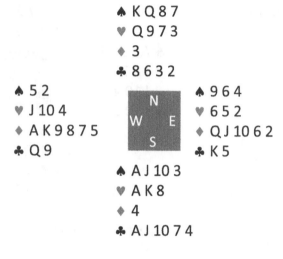

	♠ K Q 8 7	
	♥ Q 9 7 3	
	♦ 3	
	♣ 8 6 3 2	

♠ 5 2		♠ 9 6 4
♥ J 10 4		♥ 6 5 2
♦ A K 9 8 7 5		♦ Q J 10 6 2
♣ Q 9		♣ K 5

	♠ A J 10 3	
	♥ A K 8	
	♦ 4	
	♣ A J 10 7 4	

West	North	East	South
			1 ♣
1 ♦	Dbl	2 ♦	4 ♠
Pass	Pass	Pass	

North's double is a negative double. Since two minors have been bid, his double shows both majors.

South jumps to 4♠ to show a spade fit and a hand that evaluates to 18+ points in support of spades.

Negative Double

Board 8
West Deals
None Vul

```
              ♠ 6 4 2
              ♥ J
              ♦ 10 9 7
              ♣ A J 9 8 5 4
♠ K 5                        ♠ Q 9 3
♥ 10 9 7 6 5 3 2      N      ♥ K 4
♦ Q J 6            W     E   ♦ A K 5 3 2
♣ 6                   S      ♣ Q 3 2
              ♠ A J 10 8 7
              ♥ A Q 8
              ♦ 8 4
              ♣ K 10 7
```

West	North	East	South
Pass	Pass	1 ♦	1 ♠
Dbl	2 ♠	Pass	Pass
3 ♥	Pass	Pass	Pass

West's double is a negative double. Since one major has been bid, West shows at least four hearts and at least six points.

When the bidding comes back to West, he is comfortable to bid 3♥.

West knows that East will envision long hearts but less than 10 points because if West had five or more hearts and 10+ points, West would have bid 2♥ over the 1♠ overcall.

In addition, East knows that West's hearts aren't very good is that West would have opened 2♥ if he had a good six-card suit with 5-10 points. Likewise, West would have opened 3♥ if he had a good seven-card suit. Eureka! West has very long hearts that aren't very good

Responsive Doubles

Responsive Doubles

A Responsive Double is a double made by Advancer (responder to overcaller). This double occurs after opener bids one of a suit, partner overcalls a suit and responder to opener raises opener's suit. Advancer promises 6+ points and at least four cards in the remaining two suits. Not the suit opened and raised, not the suit overcaller (partner) bid.

An example would be:

North	East	South	West
1♥	1♠	2♥	Dbl*

*A Responsive Double showing 6+ points and at least 4 diamonds, at least 4 clubs and less than three spades (since with three spades or more West would have raised spades).

Overcaller will "raise" one of Advancer's suits with a fit or return to his own suit at the appropriate level. Minimum bids show minimum hands. Jump with good hands etc. *With everyone bidding, this bid tends to be based more on shape (distribution) than on high card points.* Responsive Doubles have a much more competitive nature than an attempt to reach a game.

This bid may also be used if partner makes a Takeout Double and responder to opener bids a new suit, but you will need to **have a discussion with individual partners to iron out your agreement(s)**.

North	East	South	West
1♥	Dbl	2♥	Dbl

or

North	East	South	West
1♣	Dbl	1♥	Dbl

In the first auction, there would be a tendency for the Responsive Double to be for the minor suits, as West would normally bid spades with four spades.

In the second auction, suppose West had four spades and four diamonds and was more interested in finding a safe fit than necessarily a major fit. West can use a Responsive Double to find a diamond fit when his partner does not have four spades.

Responsive Double

Board 9
North Deals
E-W Vul

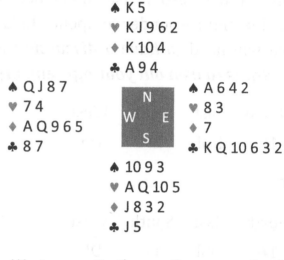

♠ K 5
♥ K J 9 6 2
♦ K 10 4
♣ A 9 4

♠ Q J 8 7
♥ 7 4
♦ A Q 9 6 5
♣ 8 7

♠ A 6 4 2
♥ 8 3
♦ 7
♣ K Q 10 6 3 2

♠ 10 9 3
♥ A Q 10 5
♦ J 8 3 2
♣ J 5

West	North	East	South
	1 ♥	2 ♣	2 ♥
Dbl	Pass	2 ♠	Pass
Pass	Pass		

West's double is a Responsive Double showing at least four cards in the two unbid suits (spades and diamonds) and a least 6 points.

Since North passed, East must bid and with a spade fit, bids 2♠.

Responsive Double

Board 10
East Deals
Both Vul

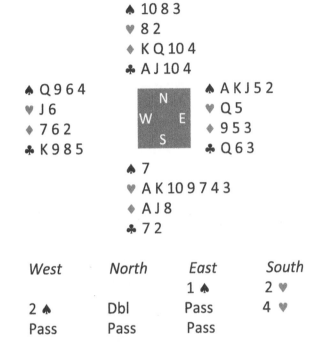

```
              ♠ 10 8 3
              ♥ 8 2
              ♦ K Q 10 4
              ♣ A J 10 4

♠ Q 9 6 4                    ♠ A K J 5 2
♥ J 6           N            ♥ Q 5
♦ 7 6 2       W   E          ♦ 9 5 3
♣ K 9 8 5       S            ♣ Q 6 3

              ♠ 7
              ♥ A K 10 9 7 4 3
              ♦ A J 8
              ♣ 7 2
```

West	North	East	South
		1 ♠	2 ♥
2 ♠	Dbl	Pass	4 ♥
Pass	Pass	Pass	

North's double is a Responsive double showing at least four cards in both minor suits and at least 6 points.

South has no fit in either minor, but does have a long heart suit so re-bids hearts. He chooses to bid game in hearts since he knows that North has some value and that the points North has will most likely be in clubs and diamonds.

Snapdragon Doubles

Snapdragon Doubles

A Snapdragon Double is a type of takeout double made by Advancer. It occurs when three suits have been bid and he (advancer) is the fourth person to make a bid. It shows the unbid suit (usually 5+ cards), 6-9 points and typically, a tolerance (two cards) in partner's overcalled suit if it was a major suit and a fit if partner overcalled a minor.

The difference in the two treatments is the level at which you expect to compete and the fact that if partner had overcalled a major and you had a fit, you would have simply raised partner's major suit.

An example would be:

North	East	South	West
1♥	2♣	2♦	Dbl

Double would promise 6+ points, 4+ spades and at least a tolerance (A, K or Q and a small card or 3+ cards) for clubs.

and;

North	East	South	West
1♦	1♠	2♣	Dbl

Double would promise 6+ points, 5+ hearts and deny a fit for spades. West is expected to have a tolerance (two spades) for spades. Remember that if West had 3+ spades and knew they already had a major fit, he would simply raise partner's major.

Note: In both examples, if West bid his suit directly he would show a five-card or longer suit and 10+ points.

Snapdragon

Board 11
South Deals
None Vul

<pre>
                   ♠ 7 4
                   ♥ Q 7 5
                   ♦ A Q 9 8 7 6 2
                   ♣ Q
      ♠ 9 6   ♠ A 10 8 3
      ♥ 9 8 6 3   N   ♥ K J 10 4 2
      ♦ K 5   W   E   ♦ 10
      ♣ A K 10 5 4   S   ♣ 8 7 6
                   ♠ K Q J 5 2
                   ♥ A
                   ♦ J 4 3
                   ♣ J 9 3 2
</pre>

West	North	East	South
			1 ♠
2 ♣	2 ♦	Dbl	Pass
2 ♥	Pass	Pass	Pass

East's double is Snapdragon showing the unbid (fourth) suit - hearts - and at least 6 points.

With a fit in hearts West bids 2♥.

Snapdragon

Board 12
West Deals
N-S Vul

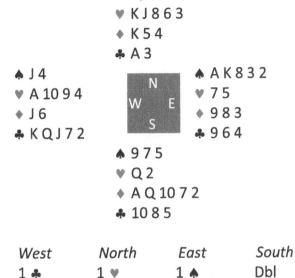

♠ Q 10 6
♥ K J 8 6 3
♦ K 5 4
♣ A 3

♠ J 4
♥ A 10 9 4
♦ J 6
♣ K Q J 7 2

♠ A K 8 3 2
♥ 7 5
♦ 9 8 3
♣ 9 6 4

♠ 9 7 5
♥ Q 2
♦ A Q 10 7 2
♣ 10 8 5

West	North	East	South
1 ♣	1 ♥	1 ♠	Dbl
Pass	1 N	Pass	Pass
Pass			

South's double is Snapdragon, showing the unbid (fourth) suit and at least 6 point.

Though North has a fit with diamonds, he also has a stopper in all the other suits so chooses to bid NT and try for a bigger score than bidding 2♦.

Balancing Doubles

Balancing Doubles

A Balancing Double is a takeout double made by overcaller. Balancing Doubles are generally thought to occur when an opponent opens the bidding and the auction comes around to you at a low level. The primary motivating factor in balancing is to force the opponents to bid to a higher level in order to win the contract. Hopefully they will bid high enough that you have an opportunity to set them.

The premise is that it is almost never right to allow the opponents to play at a low level when you have shortness in their suit. In all of the auctions below, notice that the opponents have limited their hands to minimum values and the expectation is that East/West have at least half of the high card points available in the hand. Double allows East/West to enter the auction as safely as possible and to find their best fit.

Hand 1

North	East	South	West
1♥	Pass	Pass	Dbl

Double is a Balancing Double for takeout (asking partner to bid), but could be weaker than the values a Takeout Double would have shown in the direct seat (East was in the direct seat.).

Hand 2

North	East	South	West
1♥	Pass	2♥	Pass
Pass	Dbl		

Double is a Balancing Double for takeout (asking partner to bid), but since East did not double in direct seat (his first opportunity to double), it is either weaker (less than 11 points) or off-shape (not the expected distribution of shortness in hearts and at least three cards in the remaining three suits).

Hand 3

North	East	South	West
1♥	Pass	1♠	Pass
1N	Dbl		

Double is a Balancing Double, asking partner to bid one of the minor suits but could be weaker hand than a Takeout Double would have shown in direct seat (Direct seat would have been at East's first opportunity to double.)

Hand 4

North	East	South	West
1♥	Pass	1♠	Pass
1N	Pass	Pass	Dbl

Double is takeout for the minor suits but weaker than Hand 3, since West could have doubled 1♠ showing the minors if he had the required values to double at his first opportunity to bid.

A balancing double can be made with as few as 8 HCPs depending on:

- The shape of your hand;
- The level at which partner will have to bid;
- Whether the opponents have discovered a fit;
- The vulnerability; and
- Your nerve.

Shape: The more perfect your shape (4-4-4-1 or 5-4-4-0 or 5-4-2-2), the more aggressive you should be when deciding whether to balance.

Level: The higher the level at which you are forcing partner to bid, the stronger your hand should be in either high card points or shape.

Fit: If the opponents have discovered a fit, it is generally safer to balance as they are more likely to bid one more time and there is more "room" for partner to have a fit with one of your suits.

Vulnerability: The safest time to balance is when no one is vulnerable. The opponents are less likely to double you and are more likely to compete. Remember that down one, doubled, not vulnerable is only 100 points. That is less than what they expect to score in a part-score, therefore, they are more likely to compete.

Nerve: What is your style? Pushing the opponents up one level will increase your chances of setting their contract and that is, generally, the purpose for balancing. You really don't expect (nor want) to win the contract. . .you just want them to bid one more time. You need to look confident and assured when you balance. Both you and partner should look like you expect to make your bid.

Almost everyone would rather declare than defend. Be careful. When partner has balanced don't punish partner for bidding with weaker values. Your goal was to push them to a higher level. When they bid one more time, your job is done!

Balancing Double

Board 13
North Deals
Both Vul

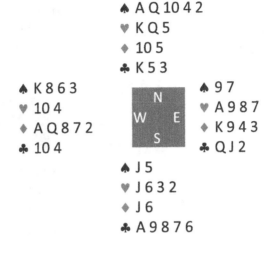

♠ A Q 10 4 2
♥ K Q 5
♦ 10 5
♣ K 5 3

♠ K 8 6 3
♥ 10 4
♦ A Q 8 7 2
♣ 10 4

♠ 9 7
♥ A 9 8 7
♦ K 9 4 3
♣ Q J 2

♠ J 5
♥ J 6 3 2
♦ J 6
♣ A 9 8 7 6

West	North	East	South
	1 ♠	Pass	1 N
Pass	Pass	Dbl	Pass
2 ♦	Pass	Pass	Pass

East's double is a Balancing Double. East's hand was too weak to double initially. Doubling now shows a hand that does not want the opponents to play 1NT. West bids as cheaply as possible, since he knows they cannot have the values to try for game.

Balancing Double

Board 14
East Deals
None Vul

	♠ A 10 9 4	
	♥ A J 5 3	
	♦ 9 6 2	
	♣ 9 7	

♠ 8 7 2		♠ K 5 3
♥ K 4 2	N	♥ 10
♦ K J 10 4	W E	♦ Q 7 3
♣ Q 10 6	S	♣ A K J 8 4 3

	♠ Q J 6	
	♥ Q 9 8 7 6	
	♦ A 8 5	
	♣ 5 2	

West	North	East	South
		1 ♣	Pass
1 N	Pass	2 ♣	Pass
Pass	Dbl	Pass	2 ♥
Pass	Pass	Pass	

North's double is a Balancing Double. If North had held shortness in clubs, 11+ points and at least three cards in each of the remaining three suits, he would have doubled over 1NT. Doubling, after his original pass, shows a hand that was either too weak to bid the first time or a hand who's distribution was "off."

Re-opening Doubles

Re-opening Doubles

A Re-opening Double is a double that can be bid by anyone, but is primarily associated with the opening bidder. A Re-opening Double occurs when you have either the maximum for your initial bid or a better hand than partner expects and the opponents have competed in the auction. Double is a flexible bid that allows partner to be in on the decision making process, deciding whether to bid or double the opponents for penalty. You may also hear this referred to as an "Action Double". It is basically a double that asks partner to "do something intelligent".

Some examples:

Hand 1

North	East	South	West
1♥	1♠	Pass	Pass
Dbl			

North should have *(remember that if South had doubled, his bid would have been a Negative Double. It is possible that South has good hand with long, good spades and would like to penalize East. Not likely, but possible.)*:

The double by North shows:

- Shortness in spades;
- Five hearts, at least three clubs and at least three diamonds; and
- A solid (12+ points) opening bid.

Hand 2

North	East	South	West
1♥	1♠	2♥	Pass
Pass	Dbl		

The double by East shows:

- Shortness in hearts (0-1-2);
- Five spades, at least three clubs and at least three diamonds; and
- 15-17 points (the best hand his partner could expect him to have given the auction).

Hand 3

North	East	South	West
1♣	Dbl	1♠	2♥
Pass	Pass	Dbl	

The double by South shows:

- Five or less spades;
- 10+ points;

- Three or four clubs; and
- Three or more diamonds.

In general a Re-Opening Double is a double made when a player:

- Has not limited his hand to a minimum range of points; and
- Has not found a fit with partner.

In the hand below, North/South have found a heart fit. North could have competed to 3♥, bid game in hearts, bid a Help Suit Game Try or passed. North's double is penalty oriented.

North	East	South	West
1♥	Pass	2♥	2♠
Dbl			

This is **NOT** a re-opening double. This is a penalty double. North should have:

- Three or more spades with an honor (if only three spades usually two honors);
- Only five hearts; and
- A hand strong enough that he expects to set West in 2♠.

Re-opening Double

Board 15
South Deals
N-S Vul

```
              ♠ 5 2
              ♥ J 10 3
              ♦ Q J 8 6 5
              ♣ 6 3 2

 ♠ J 10 3           N          ♠ Q 9 4
 ♥ K Q 7        W       E      ♥ 9 8 6 2
 ♦ 9                S          ♦ 4 3 2
 ♣ A K 10 9 8 5               ♣ Q J 4

              ♠ A K 8 7 6
              ♥ A 5 4
              ♦ A K 10 7
              ♣ 7
```

West	North	East	South
			1 ♠
2 ♣	Pass	Pass	Dbl
Pass	2 ♦	Pass	3 ♦
Pass	Pass	Pass	

South's double is a Re-opening Double showing shortness in clubs, at least three cards in the two unbid suits and a solid opening hand.

After North's 2♦ bid, South raises to 3♦ to show a very good hand (17+).

Remember that if North had bid initially over 2♣, he would have shown 10+ points and 5+ diamonds so it was possible that North could have had a decent hand, just not enough to bid over 2♣.

Re-opening Double
Board 16
West Deals
E-W Vul

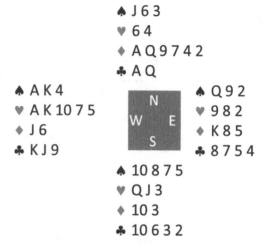

```
                   ♠ J 6 3
                   ♥ 6 4
                   ♦ A Q 9 7 4 2
                   ♣ A Q
        ♠ A K 4              ♠ Q 9 2
        ♥ A K 10 7 5         ♥ 9 8 2
        ♦ J 6                ♦ K 8 5
        ♣ K J 9              ♣ 8 7 5 4
                   ♠ 10 8 7 5
                   ♥ Q J 3
                   ♦ 10 3
                   ♣ 10 6 3 2
```

West	North	East	South
1 ♥	2 ♦	Pass	Pass
Dbl	Pass	2 ♥	Pass
Pass	Pass		

West's double is a Re-opening Double showing shortness in diamonds, at least three cards in each of the unbid suits and a solid opening bid.

After East bids 2♥, West passes.

Remember that East did not bid 2♥ over 2♦. East does not have as many as six points. If East does not have six points, West does not envision that they can make game as he has a balanced hand with at least six losers: one spade, one heart, two diamonds and two (or three) clubs.

Support Doubles

Support Doubles

Support Doubles, created by Eric Rodwell, is one of the most useful doubles in bridge. It is a double made by opener, after an opponent has overcalled a suit. It is used to show three-card support for the suit bid by responder. The premise behind a Support Double is that opener is unlikely to have a hand that wanted to make a penalty double of the opponent's suit at the two-level. Since that is unlikely, let's use the double to convey information that may be valuable to our side.

Example:

North	East	South	West
1♣	P	1♥	1♠
Dbl *			

* A "Support Double" promising three hearts

Here are the rules concerning Support Doubles:

- Opener must have opened one of some suit;
- Responder must have bid one of some suit;
- It is unlimited in high card values (though of course opener has an opening hand);
- It shows exactly three card support;

- It does not deny length in any other suit, nor promise shortness in any other suit;
- It can only be made when the suit overcalled is below the two level of the suit responder bid; and
- It can also be a "Support Redouble" if the overcall was the bid "double".

Opener's bid must have been 1♣/1♦/1♥/1♠ - Support Doubles are not made unless opener's first bid was a one-level suit bid.

Responder's bid must have been 1♦/1♥/1♠ - Support Doubles are not made unless responder's first bid was a one-level suit bid.

Unlimited High Card Values–the Support Double can be made with an 11-point hand or up to a 20-point hand. Responder is not allowed to pass the support double (unless his right hand opponent bids) so opener will always have another opportunity to show the value of his hand.

Exactly Three Card Support – with four or more cards in responder's suit simply raise to the appropriate level. With less than three cards in responder's suit simply make your most natural bid...which may be pass.

No Length or Shortness is Promised in any Other Suit – opener may have a four-card major or a five-card minor (or longer). Opener's Support Double simply says, I have three cards in responder's suit. Since responder must bid after the double, opener will have other opportunities to show his length in other suits if needed.

The Overcall Must be Below the Two Level of Responder's Suit – since responder may end up playing a seven-card fit in some instances, opener would not want to force the responder to play at the three level. Therefore, the overcall must allow responder to be able to bid his suit at the two level. Two examples:

North	East	South	West
1♣	P	1♥	2♦
Dbl *			

*A Support Double since South could bid 2♥ over the 2♦ bid.

North	East	South	West
1♣	P	1♥	2♠
Dbl **			

**<u>Not</u> a support double as South would be forced to the three level if he wanted to bid hearts.

Support Redoubles can also be used – if an opponent's overcall was a takeout double, then a bid by opener of "Redouble" is a "Support Redouble" and shows three-card support for responder's suit. An Example:

North	East	South	West
1♣	P	1♥	Dbl
Re-Dbl *			

*A Support Redouble promising exactly three hearts.

Responder's 2nd Bid after a Support Double (or Redouble) by Opener

When you have Five or More Cards in the Major Suit in which you Responded: This is the easiest situation to handle. When opener has promised three-card support for your major and you know you have a fit...simply do the math.

- Bid at the two level when you have 6-bad 10 points.
- Jump to the three-level and invite game with a good 10-12 points.

- Bid game when you know you have the values for game 13+ points.

When you have Only Four Cards in the Major Suit in which you Responded:

- With weak (6-10 HCPs) hands **when your RHO has passed:**
    - Either bid two of your major and play your seven card fit;
    - Return to opener's minor suit at the lowest level with four or more cards in his minor; or
    - Bid 1NT with a stopper in the suit the opponent bid and a balanced hand.
- With weak (6-10 HCPs) hands **when your RHO has bid:**
    - Return to opener's minor suit at the lowest level with five or more cards in his minor; or
    - Pass.
- With better (10-12 HCPs) hands **whether your RHO has passed or bid:**
    - Either bid two of your major and play your seven card fit; or
    - Bid a new suit (which is forcing one round); or

- Return to opener's minor suit skipping a level with four or more cards in his minor; or
- Bid 2NT with a stopper in the suit the opponent bid and a balanced hand.
- With game forcing (13+ HCPs) hands **whether your RHO has passed or bid:**
  - Either cue-bid the opponent's suit; or
  - Bid a new suit (which is forcing one round); or
  - Bid 3NT with a stopper in the suit the opponent bid and a balanced hand.

Opener's Third Bid: At this point your bidding is very normal...with only one exception. Opener must remember that, when your LHO has passed, *if responder bids the suit you supported at the two-level he does not promise that you have discovered a fit*. He may simply be trying to stay as low and safe as possible.

The value of this bid is tremendous. In competitive auctions it is a huge benefit to know how many cards opener has in your suit. In the following hands we'll look at some examples of what you might hold and how the information you received influences your subsequent bids.

Support Doubles

Board 1
North Deals
None Vul

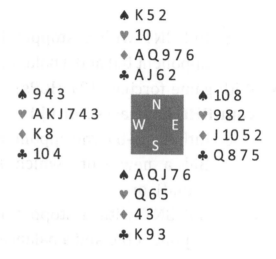

	♠ K 5 2	
	♥ 10	
	♦ A Q 9 7 6	
	♣ A J 6 2	

♠ 9 4 3
♥ A K J 7 4 3
♦ K 8
♣ 10 4

♠ 10 8
♥ 9 8 2
♦ J 10 5 2
♣ Q 8 7 5

♠ A Q J 7 6
♥ Q 6 5
♦ 4 3
♣ K 9 3

West	North	East	South
	1 ♦	Pass	1 ♠
2 ♥	Dbl	Pass	3 ♠
Pass	4 ♠	Pass	Pass
Pass			

North's double is a Support Double showing three card spade support.

With five spades and invitational values South jumps to 3♠.

North bids game.

Support Doubles

East Deals
N-S Vul

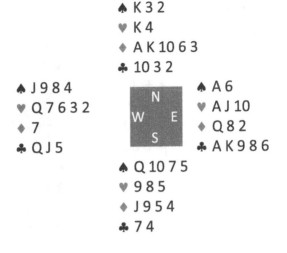

♠ K 3 2
♥ K 4
♦ A K 10 6 3
♣ 10 3 2

♠ J 9 8 4
♥ Q 7 6 3 2
♦ 7
♣ Q J 5

♠ A 6
♥ A J 10
♦ Q 8 2
♣ A K 9 8 6

♠ Q 10 7 5
♥ 9 8 5
♦ J 9 5 4
♣ 7 4

West	North	East	South
		1 ♣	Pass
1 ♥	2 ♦	Dbl	Pass
2 ♥	Pass	3 N	Pass
4 ♥	Pass	Pass	Pass

East's double is a Support Double showing three card support for hearts.

West with five hearts and a weak hand, simply bids 2♥.

East now bids 3NT to show the values for game with a diamond stopper.

West corrects to 4♥ since they have an eight-card heart fit.

Support Doubles

Board 3
South Deals
E-W Vul

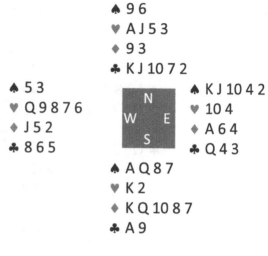

	♠ 9 6		
	♥ A J 5 3		
	♦ 9 3		
	♣ K J 10 7 2		

♠ 5 3		♠ K J 10 4 2
♥ Q 9 8 7 6		♥ 10 4
♦ J 5 2		♦ A 6 4
♣ 8 6 5		♣ Q 4 3

	♠ A Q 8 7	
	♥ K 2	
	♦ K Q 10 8 7	
	♣ A 9	

West	North	East	South
			1 ♦
Pass	1 ♥	2 ♠	Dbl
Pass	Pass	Pass	

South's double is not a Support Double since 2♠ is above the level of 2♥.

South's double is a Penalty Double.

Support Doubles

Board 4
West Deals
Both Vul

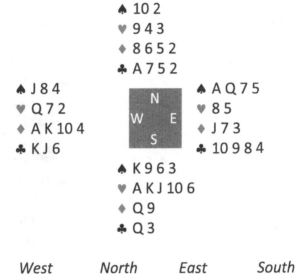

	♠ 10 2	
	♥ 9 4 3	
	♦ 8 6 5 2	
	♣ A 7 5 2	

♠ J 8 4
♥ Q 7 2
♦ A K 10 4
♣ K J 6

♠ A Q 7 5
♥ 8 5
♦ J 7 3
♣ 10 9 8 4

♠ K 9 6 3
♥ A K J 10 6
♦ Q 9
♣ Q 3

West	North	East	South
1 ♦	Pass	1 ♠	2 ♥
Dbl	Pass	2 ♠	Pass
Pass	Pass		

Though East does not have five spades, he has a weak hand with no fit for partner's minor. East simply bids 2♠ to stay low and safe.

Support Doubles

Board 5
North Deals
N-S Vul

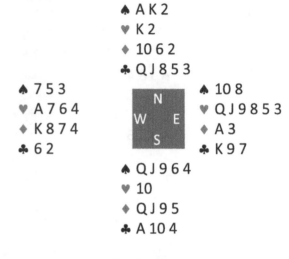

North
♠ A K 2
♥ K 2
♦ 10 6 2
♣ Q J 8 5 3

West
♠ 7 5 3
♥ A 7 6 4
♦ K 8 7 4
♣ 6 2

East
♠ 10 8
♥ Q J 9 8 5 3
♦ A 3
♣ K 9 7

South
♠ Q J 9 6 4
♥ 10
♦ Q J 9 5
♣ A 10 4

West	North	East	South
	1 ♣	1 ♥	1 ♠
2 ♥	Dbl	Pass	3 ♠
Pass	4 ♠	Pass	Pass
Pass			

North's double is a Support Double showing three card support for spades. South has an invitational hand with five spades so jumps to 3♠.

When South jumps to 3♠, South guarantees at least five spades.

Support Doubles

Board 6
East Deals
E-W Vul

```
                    ♠ A K J 6 3
                    ♥ Q 7 3
                    ♦ 9 7 3
                    ♣ K 3
```

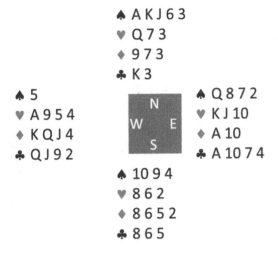

```
♠ 5                          ♠ Q 8 7 2
♥ A 9 5 4                    ♥ K J 10
♦ K Q J 4                    ♦ A 10
♣ Q J 9 2                    ♣ A 10 7 4

                    ♠ 10 9 4
                    ♥ 8 6 2
                    ♦ 8 6 5 2
                    ♣ 8 6 5
```

West	North	East	South
		1 ♣	Pass
1 ♥	1 ♠	Dbl	Pass
2 ♦	Pass	2 N	Pass
3 N	Pass	Pass	Pass

East's double is a Support Double showing three card support in hearts.

With only four hearts but an opening hand, West wants to force partner to bid again. 2♦, a new suit by responder, forces East to bid one more time.

East now shows a stopper in the spade suit, West bids game.

Support Doubles

Board 7
South Deals
Both Vul

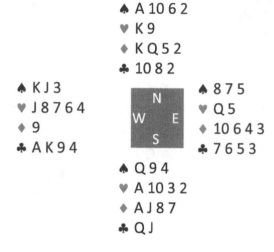

```
                    ♠ A 10 6 2
                    ♥ K 9
                    ♦ K Q 5 2
                    ♣ 10 8 2
   ♠ K J 3                        ♠ 8 7 5
   ♥ J 8 7 6 4          N         ♥ Q 5
   ♦ 9              W       E      ♦ 10 6 4 3
   ♣ A K 9 4            S          ♣ 7 6 5 3
                    ♠ Q 9 4
                    ♥ A 10 3 2
                    ♦ A J 8 7
                    ♣ Q J
```

West	North	East	South
			1 ♦
Pass	1 ♠	2 ♥	Dbl
Pass	2 N	Pass	3 N
Pass	Pass	Pass	

South's double is a Support Double showing three card support in spades.

North does not have five spades but does have a good hand with a stopper in hearts, so bids 2NT showing 11-12 points and a heart stopper, denying five spades.

Support Doubles

Board 8
West Deals
None Vul

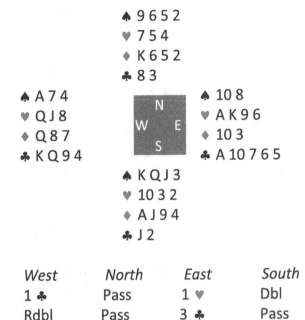

<table>
<tr><td>♠ 9 6 5 2</td></tr>
<tr><td>♥ 7 5 4</td></tr>
<tr><td>♦ K 6 5 2</td></tr>
<tr><td>♣ 8 3</td></tr>
</table>

West	North	East	South
1 ♣	Pass	1 ♥	Dbl
Rdbl	Pass	3 ♣	Pass
Pass	Pass		

West's redouble is a Support Redouble showing three hearts.

East has only four hearts, but has an invitational hand with clubs so jumps to 3♣.

Support Doubles

Board 9
North Deals
E-W Vul

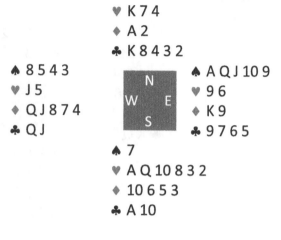

```
                    ♠ K 6 2
                    ♥ K 7 4
                    ♦ A 2
                    ♣ K 8 4 3 2

    ♠ 8 5 4 3              N          ♠ A Q J 10 9
    ♥ J 5             W         E     ♥ 9 6
    ♦ Q J 8 7 4                       ♦ K 9
    ♣ Q J                 S           ♣ 9 7 6 5

                    ♠ 7
                    ♥ A Q 10 8 3 2
                    ♦ 10 6 5 3
                    ♣ A 10
```

West	North	East	South
	1 ♣	1 ♠	2 ♥
2 ♠	3 ♥	Pass	4 ♥
Pass	Pass	Pass	

Since South's 2♥ bid shows five or more hearts, North can bid 3♥ over 2♠ with only three hearts.

North would not have been able to make a Support Double as 2♠ is above the two-level in responder's suit (hearts).

Support Doubles

Board 10
East Deals
Both Vul

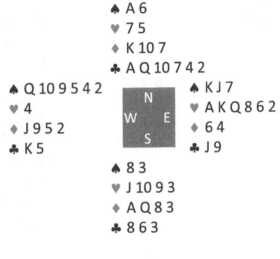

♠ A 6
♥ 7 5
♦ K 10 7
♣ A Q 10 7 4 2

♠ Q 10 9 5 4 2
♥ 4
♦ J 9 5 2
♣ K 5

♠ K J 7
♥ A K Q 8 6 2
♦ 6 4
♣ J 9

♠ 8 3
♥ J 10 9 3
♦ A Q 8 3
♣ 8 6 3

West	North	East	South
		1 ♥	Pass
1 ♠	2 ♣	Dbl	3 ♣
3 ♠	Pass	Pass	Pass

East's double is a Support Double showing three card spade support.

West competes to 3♠.

Support Doubles

Board 11

South Deals
None Vul

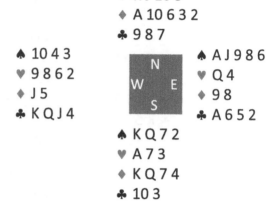

♠ 5
♥ K J 10 5
♦ A 10 6 3 2
♣ 9 8 7

♠ 10 4 3
♥ 9 8 6 2
♦ J 5
♣ K Q J 4

♠ A J 9 8 6
♥ Q 4
♦ 9 8
♣ A 6 5 2

♠ K Q 7 2
♥ A 7 3
♦ K Q 7 4
♣ 10 3

West	North	East	South
			1 ♦
Pass	1 ♥	1 ♠	Dbl
2 ♠	3 ♦	Pass	Pass
Pass			

South's double is a Support Double showing three card heart support.

North does not want to play in hearts, but has support for South's diamonds so bids 3♦.

Support Doubles

Board 12
West Deals
N-S Vul

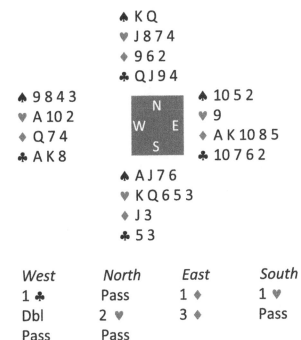

♠ K Q
♥ J 8 7 4
♦ 9 6 2
♣ Q J 9 4

♠ 9 8 4 3
♥ A 10 2
♦ Q 7 4
♣ A K 8

♠ 10 5 2
♥ 9
♦ A K 10 8 5
♣ 10 7 6 2

♠ A J 7 6
♥ K Q 6 5 3
♦ J 3
♣ 5 3

West	North	East	South
1 ♣	Pass	1 ♦	1 ♥
Dbl	2 ♥	3 ♦	Pass
Pass	Pass		

West's double is a Support Double showing three card diamond support.

East competes to 3♦.

Maximal Doubles

Maximal Doubles

A Maximal Double is a bid made after you and partner have bid and raised a major suit and your right hand opponent (RHO) has overcalled the suit directly in rank below your major suit. Two examples:

North	East	South	West	**OR**	North	East	South	West
1♥	2♦	2♥	3♦		1♠	2♥	2♠	3♥

In each case the opponents have bid the suit directly in rank below your major suit. A "double" by North would be a Maximal Double indicating that he is considering game, but does not have a hand strong enough to make game if South is on the low end (6-7 points) of his minimum response.

Why should you play this? What advantage does it give you? *Why should North not just bid 3♥ or 3♠?*

Suppose North had the hand below, he and partner (South) have bid and raised spades and his opponent competed to 3♥.

North	East	South	West
1♠	2♥	2♠	3♥
?			

♠AKJ542 ♥2 ♦1098 ♣K32 wouldn't North want to compete to 3♠? North would not want to invite game, but he would certainly want to compete for the part-score opportunity.

But suppose North had this hand:

♠AQJ54 ♥76 ♦AQ75 ♣K8 now North would want to bid 3♠, asking South to bid game with a good hand.

How would South know which type of hand North holds? These hands are why Maximal Doubles were created. You can't do both...not unless you play Maximal Doubles.

Once you add Maximal Doubles, a bid of 3♠ becomes a competitive bid saying, "I don't want the opponents to take the bid from us" and double says, "I'm interested in playing game but I need to know what you think partner? Are you at the top or bottom of your 2♠ bid?"

If the opponents compete in a suit more than one rank below your suit, you can use a Help Suit Game Try to show interest in game. It's only when they bid the suit directly below your major suit that a Maximal Double is used.

Responder's (South's) Bid

What does responder bid after opener's (North's) bid?

If North bids 3♥ or 3♠, South will pass. North did not make a try for game. North was simply competing for the part-score.

If North bids "double" (a Maximal Double), then South will evaluate his hand for game.

If South has:

- 6-7 points, he will return to the major suit at the three level;
- 8-9 points, he will bid game in their major suit; or
- A hand that he feels has a good chance for game due to his distribution or trick taking ability, he will bid game in their major suit.

What type of hand, without maximum points, would South feel he has the ability to make game? In the following auction:

North	East	South	West
1♠	2♥	2♠	3♥

Dbl (Maximal)

If South held the hand below, he would bid game.

♠Q542 ♥32 ♦108 ♣A10932

Extra (4 cards) trump length, shortness in hearts, a second five card suit with an honor (clubs), primary cards (♠Q and ♣A); all of these things should help South evaluate to game, regardless of his HCPs.

The following hands explore when to bid:

- 3♥ or 3♠ to simply compete for the auction when you know your partnership does not have the values for game, or
- A Maximal Double, when you know that you and partner are close to the values (or tricks for game),or
- A Help Suit Game Try, when you know that you and partner are close to the values (or tricks for game), or
- 4♥ or 4♠, when you know your partnership has the values for game.

Maximal Doubles

Board 1

North Deals
None Vul

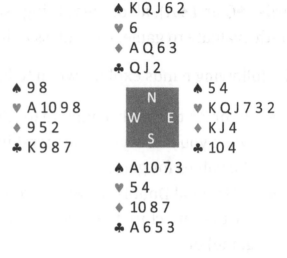

Spades K Q J 6 2
Hearts 6
Diamonds A Q 6 3
Clubs Q J 2

Spades 9 8
Hearts A 10 9 8
Diamonds 9 5 2
Clubs K 9 8 7

Spades 5 4
Hearts K Q J 7 3 2
Diamonds K J 4
Clubs 10 4

Spades A 10 7 3
Hearts 5 4
Diamonds 10 8 7
Clubs A 6 5 3

West	North	East	South
	1 ♠	2 ♥	2 ♠
3 ♥	Dbl	Pass	4 ♠
Pass	Pass	Pass	

Double is a *Maximal Double.*

Dbl = A Maximal Double showing a hand interested in bidding game in spades if partner is at the top of their 2♠ raise.

4♠ = I have 8-9 points.

Maximal Doubles

Board 2

East Deals
N-S Vul

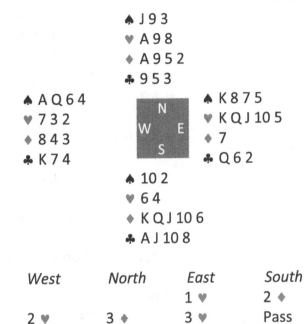

	♠ J 9 3	
	♥ A 9 8	
	♦ A 9 5 2	
	♣ 9 5 3	

♠ A Q 6 4		♠ K 8 7 5
♥ 7 3 2		♥ K Q J 10 5
♦ 8 4 3		♦ 7
♣ K 7 4		♣ Q 6 2

	♠ 10 2	
	♥ 6 4	
	♦ K Q J 10 6	
	♣ A J 10 8	

West	North	East	South
		1 ♥	2 ♦
2 ♥	3 ♦	3 ♥	Pass
Pass	Pass		

A competitive bid.

3♥ = A competitive bid. East simply wants to compete for the contract.

Maximal Doubles

Board 3
South Deals
E-W Vul

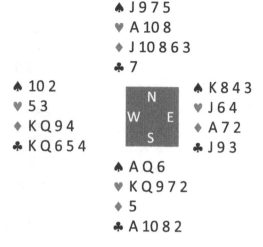

```
                        ♠ J 9 7 5
                        ♥ A 10 8
                        ♦ J 10 8 6 3
                        ♣ 7
        ♠ 10 2                          ♠ K 8 4 3
        ♥ 5 3              N            ♥ J 6 4
        ♦ K Q 9 4      W       E        ♦ A 7 2
        ♣ K Q 6 5 4        S            ♣ J 9 3
                        ♠ A Q 6
                        ♥ K Q 9 7 2
                        ♦ 5
                        ♣ A 10 8 2
```

West	North	East	South
			1 ♥
2 ♣	2 ♥	3 ♣	Dbl
Pass	Pass	Pass	

A Penalty Double.

Dbl = A Penalty Double. If South had wanted to invite game
he would have bid 3♦, a Help Suit Game Try. *Remember, for
a double to be a Maximal Double, the suit bid must have
been the one directly in rank below your suit.*

Maximal Doubles

Board 4
West Deals
Both Vul

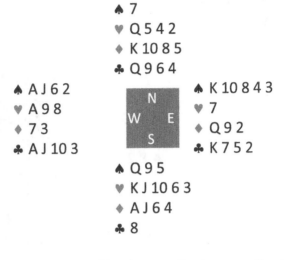

♠ 7
♥ Q 5 4 2
♦ K 10 8 5
♣ Q 9 6 4

♠ A J 6 2
♥ A 9 8
♦ 7 3
♣ A J 10 3

♠ K 10 8 4 3
♥ 7
♦ Q 9 2
♣ K 7 5 2

♠ Q 9 5
♥ K J 10 6 3
♦ A J 6 4
♣ 8

West	North	East	South
1 ♣	Pass	1 ♠	2 ♥
2 ♠	3 ♥	3 ♠	Pass
Pass	Pass		

A Competitive Bid.

3♠ = A competitive bid simply wanting to compete for the contract. East would have made a Maximal Double if he had wanted to make a try for game.

Maximal Doubles

Board 5
North Deals
N-S Vul

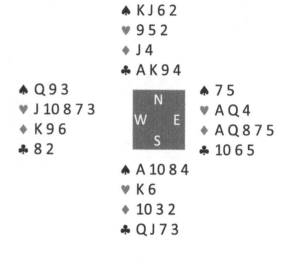

♠ K J 6 2
♥ 9 5 2
♦ J 4
♣ A K 9 4

♠ Q 9 3
♥ J 10 8 7 3
♦ K 9 6
♣ 8 2

♠ 7 5
♥ A Q 4
♦ A Q 8 7 5
♣ 10 6 5

♠ A 10 8 4
♥ K 6
♦ 10 3 2
♣ Q J 7 3

West	North	East	South
	1 ♣	1 ♦	1 ♠
2 ♦	2 ♠	3 ♦	3 ♥
Pass	3 ♠	Pass	Pass
Pass			

A Help Suit Game Try.

3 ♥ = A Help Suit Game Try. It is the only bid available
between 3 ♦ and 3 ♠ so it simply shows a general interest
in game.

Maximal Doubles

Board 6
East Deals
E-W Vul

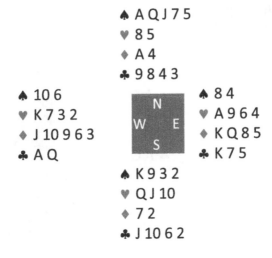

```
              ♠ A Q J 7 5
              ♥ 8 5
              ♦ A 4
              ♣ 9 8 4 3

♠ 10 6                      ♠ 8 4
♥ K 7 3 2          N        ♥ A 9 6 4
♦ J 10 9 6 3   W       E    ♦ K Q 8 5
♣ A Q             S         ♣ K 7 5

              ♠ K 9 3 2
              ♥ Q J 10
              ♦ 7 2
              ♣ J 10 6 2
```

West	North	East	South
		1 ♦	Pass
1 ♥	1 ♠	2 ♥	2 ♠
3 ♦	Pass	4 ♠	Pass
Pass	Pass		

A Help Suit Game Try.

3♦ = A Help Suit Game Try. Since West could have bid 3♣ or
3♦ to make a game try, the implication is that he does not
need help in clubs.

4♠ = "Yes, I have help in diamonds."

Maximal Doubles

Board 7
South Deals
Both Vul

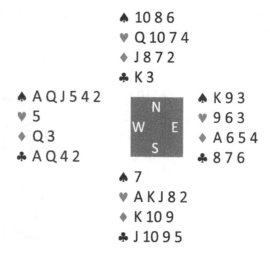

♠ 10 8 6
♥ Q 10 7 4
♦ J 8 7 2
♣ K 3

♠ A Q J 5 4 2
♥ 5
♦ Q 3
♣ A Q 4 2

♠ K 9 3
♥ 9 6 3
♦ A 6 5 4
♣ 8 7 6

♠ 7
♥ A K J 8 2
♦ K 10 9
♣ J 10 9 5

West	North	East	South
			1 ♥
1 ♠	2 ♥	2 ♠	3 ♥
4 ♠	Pass	Pass	Pass

West has the values for game, so simply bids game in spades.

Maximal Double

Board 8
West Deals
None Vul

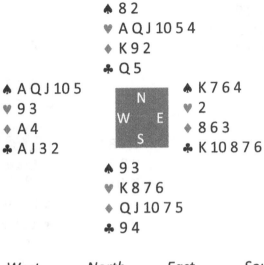

♠ 8 2
♥ A Q J 10 5 4
♦ K 9 2
♣ Q 5

♠ A Q J 10 5
♥ 9 3
♦ A 4
♣ A J 3 2

♠ K 7 6 4
♥ 2
♦ 8 6 3
♣ K 10 8 7 6

♠ 9 3
♥ K 8 7 6
♦ Q J 10 7 5
♣ 9 4

West	North	East	South
1 ♠	2 ♥	2 ♠	3 ♥
Dbl	Pass	4 ♠	Pass
Pass	Pass		

West's double is a Maximal Double.

If West simply wanted to compete he would have bid 3♠.
Since 3♥ is the suit directly in rank below spades, double
becomes the only method that West has to show interest in
game.

With 6 points, a singleton heart and a fourth trump, it is easy
for East to bid game.

Maximal Doubles

Board 9
North Deals
E-W Vul

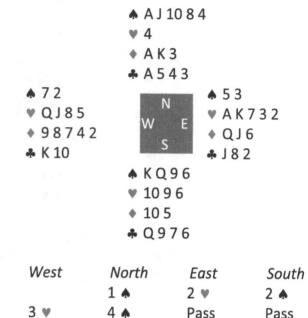

	♠ A J 10 8 4	
	♥ 4	
	♦ A K 3	
	♣ A 5 4 3	
♠ 7 2		♠ 5 3
♥ Q J 8 5		♥ A K 7 3 2
♦ 9 8 7 4 2		♦ Q J 6
♣ K 10		♣ J 8 2
	♠ K Q 9 6	
	♥ 10 9 6	
	♦ 10 5	
	♣ Q 9 7 6	

West	North	East	South
	1 ♠	2 ♥	2 ♠
3 ♥	4 ♠	Pass	Pass
Pass			

East does not make a Maximal Double to show interest in game since he already knows they have the values for game. He simply bids game.

Maximal Doubles

Board 10
North Deals
None Vul

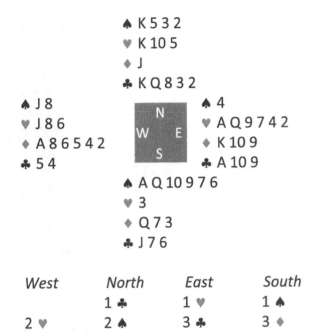

♠ K 5 3 2
♥ K 10 5
♦ J
♣ K Q 8 3 2

♠ J 8
♥ J 8 6
♦ A 8 6 5 4 2
♣ 5 4

♠ 4
♥ A Q 9 7 4 2
♦ K 10 9
♣ A 10 9

♠ A Q 10 9 7 6
♥ 3
♦ Q 7 3
♣ J 7 6

West	North	East	South
	1 ♣	1 ♥	1 ♠
2 ♥	2 ♠	3 ♣	3 ♦
Pass	4 ♠	Pass	Pass
Pass			

East's 3♣ bid is a Help Suit Game Try, asking West to bid game if he has help in clubs.

South's 3♦ bid is a game try in spades. If South was only interested in competing, he would have simply bid 3♠.

North has a singleton diamond and 4 trumps so bids game.

Maximal Doubles

Board 11

South Deals
None Vul

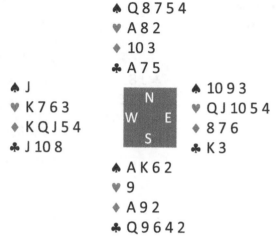

♠ Q 8 7 5 4
♥ A 8 2
♦ 10 3
♣ A 7 5

♠ J
♥ K 7 6 3
♦ K Q J 5 4
♣ J 10 8

♠ 10 9 3
♥ Q J 10 5 4
♦ 8 7 6
♣ K 3

♠ A K 6 2
♥ 9
♦ A 9 2
♣ Q 9 6 4 2

West	North	East	South
			1 ♣
1 ♦	1 ♠	2 ♦	2 ♠
3 ♦	3 ♥	Pass	4 ♠
Pass	Pass	Pass	

North's 3♥ bid is a game try in spades since the only bid between 3♦ and 3♠ is 3♥.

If North wanted to compete, he would simply have bid 3♠.

Maximal Doubles

Board 12
West Deals
N-S Vul

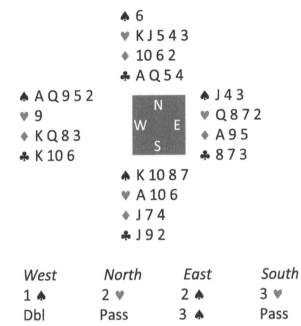

	♠ 6	
	♥ K J 5 4 3	
	♦ 10 6 2	
	♣ A Q 5 4	

♠ A Q 9 5 2
♥ 9
♦ K Q 8 3
♣ K 10 6

♠ J 4 3
♥ Q 8 7 2
♦ A 9 5
♣ 8 7 3

♠ K 10 8 7
♥ A 10 6
♦ J 7 4
♣ J 9 2

West	North	East	South
1 ♠	2 ♥	2 ♠	3 ♥
Dbl	Pass	3 ♠	Pass
Pass	Pass		

West's double is a Maximal Double asking partner to bid game in spades if they have a good hand.

East has a minimum hand, 4-3-3-3 balanced with only three trumps, so signs-off at 3♠.

Common Misconceptions

Some Common Misconceptions

There are a few mistakes and misconceptions players have concerning doubles that should be addressed.

True or False?

A Takeout Double always promises shortness in the opponents' suit unless you have 17+ points or the equivalent in trick taking ability. **True**.

Once a player has passed he can bid with less points at his second opportunity, since his partner will know that his hand is limited. **True**.

If you double, your partner has to bid. **False**. Your partner does not have to bid in two cases:

1. If partner's right hand opponent bids; or,
2. If your partner has so much strength in the opponents' suit that he believes you will get a better score by setting the opponents than by bidding. Therefore, by passing, he converts the double into a penalty double. *This almost never happens. It is right to bid around 98% of the time.*

You can bid a Takeout Double over a 1NT opening bid. **False**. Double of a NT opening bid or overcall is a penalty double.

You can bid a Takeout Double when you have a five-card suit. **True.** If you have a five-card suit that is weakish and your hand meets all other criteria you can make a Takeout Double.

One mistake that players make quite often is bidding instead of doubling. **True.** Double is a very flexible bid that pulls partner in to the decision making process. Too many times players get wrapped up in their own hand and what they think and forget that they have a partner. Anytime you are in a competitive situation and are wondering whether you should bid, make sure that you also think "I wonder if I should I double?".

Practice Hands

Competitive Doubles

Board 1
North Deals
None Vul

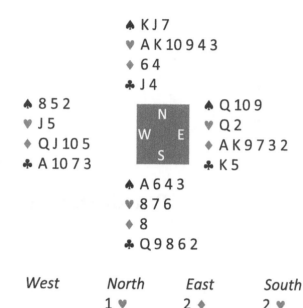

	♠ K J 7	
	♥ A K 10 9 4 3	
	♦ 6 4	
	♣ J 4	

♠ 8 5 2		♠ Q 10 9
♥ J 5		♥ Q 2
♦ Q J 10 5		♦ A K 9 7 3 2
♣ A 10 7 3		♣ K 5

	♠ A 6 4 3	
	♥ 8 7 6	
	♦ 8	
	♣ Q 9 8 6 2	

West	North	East	South
	1 ♥	2 ♦	2 ♥
3 ♦	3 ♥	Pass	Pass
Pass			

North's 3♥ bid is not invitational to game.

If North had intended to make a game try, he would have made a **Maximal Double** by doubling 3♦.

3♥ is simply a competitive bid.

Competitive Doubles

Board 2
East Deals
N-S Vul

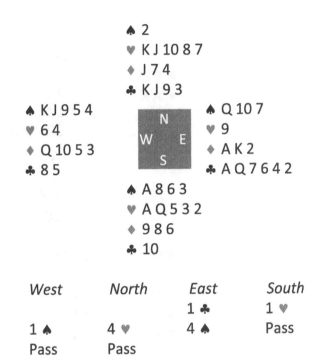

	♠ 2		
	♥ K J 10 8 7		
	♦ J 7 4		
	♣ K J 9 3		

♠ K J 9 5 4   ♠ Q 10 7
♥ 6 4   ♥ 9
♦ Q 10 5 3   ♦ A K 2
♣ 8 5   ♣ A Q 7 6 4 2

♠ A 8 6 3
♥ A Q 5 3 2
♦ 9 8 6
♣ 10

West	North	East	South
		1 ♣	1 ♥
1 ♠	4 ♥	4 ♠	Pass
Pass	Pass		

West chooses not to double, since double would be a negative double and show only four spades.

1♠ shows five spades and 6+ points.

Competitive Doubles

Board 3
South Deals
E-W Vul

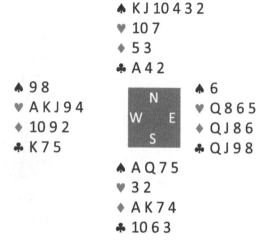

	♠ K J 10 4 3 2	
	♥ 10 7	
	♦ 5 3	
	♣ A 4 2	

♠ 9 8		♠ 6
♥ A K J 9 4		♥ Q 8 6 5
♦ 10 9 2		♦ Q J 8 6
♣ K 7 5		♣ Q J 9 8

	♠ A Q 7 5	
	♥ 3 2	
	♦ A K 7 4	
	♣ 10 6 3	

West	North	East	South
			1 ♦
1 ♥	1 ♠	2 ♥	2 ♠
3 ♥	Dbl	Pass	4 ♠
Pass	Pass	Pass	

North's double is a Maximal Double.

North's bid shows invitational values for game.

South feels that his hand has the values for game so bids 4♠.

Remember, South's 2♠ bid promised four spades as he would have made a Support Double with only three spades.

Competitive Doubles

Board 4
West Deals
E-W Vul

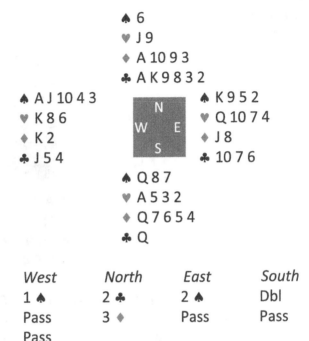

♠ 6
♥ J 9
♦ A 10 9 3
♣ A K 9 8 3 2

♠ A J 10 4 3
♥ K 8 6
♦ K 2
♣ J 5 4

♠ K 9 5 2
♥ Q 10 7 4
♦ J 8
♣ 10 7 6

♠ Q 8 7
♥ A 5 3 2
♦ Q 7 6 5 4
♣ Q

West	North	East	South
1 ♠	2 ♣	2 ♠	Dbl
Pass	3 ♦	Pass	Pass
Pass			

South's double is a Responsive Double.

South's double promises at least four diamonds and at least four hearts and the values to bid (8+ or the equivalent in shape since South is forcing partner to the three level).

North must bid since West passed and chooses his longest suit of the two partner showed.

North can choose, with some hands, to re-bid his original suit which would still only promise only five cards.

Competitive Doubles

Board 5
North Deals
N-S Vul

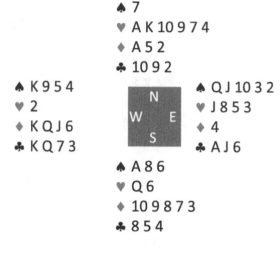

	♠ 7		
	♥ A K 10 9 7 4		
	♦ A 5 2		
	♣ 10 9 2		

♠ K 9 5 4   ♠ Q J 10 3 2
♥ 2   ♥ J 8 5 3
♦ K Q J 6   ♦ 4
♣ K Q 7 3   ♣ A J 6

♠ A 8 6
♥ Q 6
♦ 10 9 8 7 3
♣ 8 5 4

West	North	East	South
	1 ♥	Pass	1 N
Dbl	2 ♥	3 ♠	Pass
4 ♠	Pass	Pass	Pass

West's double is a Take-out Double.

West's double shows shortness in hearts (0-1-2), 11+ points and at least three cards in the remaining three suits.

East jumps in spades to show 10-11 points and spades.

West bids game.

Competitive Doubles
Board 6
East Deals
N-S Vul

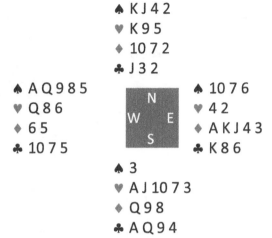

```
                    ♠ K J 4 2
                    ♥ K 9 5
                    ♦ 10 7 2
                    ♣ J 3 2
  ♠ A Q 9 8 5                      ♠ 10 7 6
  ♥ Q 8 6          N               ♥ 4 2
  ♦ 6 5         W     E            ♦ A K J 4 3
  ♣ 10 7 5         S               ♣ K 8 6
                    ♠ 3
                    ♥ A J 10 7 3
                    ♦ Q 9 8
                    ♣ A Q 9 4
```

West	North	East	South
		1 ♦	1 ♥
1 ♠	2 ♥	Dbl	3 ♥
Pass	Pass	Pass	

East's double is a Support Double.

East's double shows three card spade support.

West's pass of 3♥, denies the values to compete to the three level or higher.

East's subsequent pass, denies the values to compete to the three level or higher.

Remember, West promised 5+ spades by bidding 1♠ since, if he had only had four spades, he would have bid a Negative Double.

Competitive Doubles

Board 7
South Deals
Both Vul

	♠ Q 4 3	
	♥ K 6 4 3	
	♦ 9 6 5 3	
	♣ A 3	

♠ 10 9 6 5		♠ A K J 7 2
♥ 9 7 2	N	♥ 8
♦ 8 7	W E	♦ A Q 4
♣ 9 7 5 4	S	♣ K Q 8 6

	♠ 8	
	♥ A Q J 10 5	
	♦ K J 10 2	
	♣ J 10 2	

West	North	East	South
			1 ♥
Pass	2 ♥	2 ♠	3 ♥
Pass	Pass	Dbl	Pass
3 ♠	Pass	Pass	Pass

East's Double is a Re-opening Double.

If East passes, the auction is over and the opponents will play 3♥. East has a hand strong enough that he would like to either penalize North/South (if his partner has good hearts) or take the bid away from North/South. East is asking West to "do something intelligent".

West has no expectation that they could set 3♥ and has a spade fit so bids 3♠.

Competitive Doubles

Board 8
West Deals
None Vul

♠ A J 9 8
♥ J 10 6 5 4
♦ 6 3
♣ Q 2

	♠ K 5 3 2		♠ Q 10 6 4
	♥ 3	N	♥ A 9 8
	♦ A 8 7 5	W E	♦ Q J 4
	♣ A K 9 4	S	♣ 7 6 3

♠ 7
♥ K Q 7 2
♦ K 10 9 2
♣ J 10 8 5

West	North	East	South
1 ♦	Pass	1 ♠	Pass
2 ♠	Pass	Pass	Dbl
Pass	3 ♥	Pass	Pass
Pass			

South's double is a Balancing Double.

If South passes, the auction is over. South knows that East/West have minimum values and that he and partner have approximately half the high card points in the deck.

South doubles asking his partner to bid, showing clubs and hearts (and could also have diamonds). Even though North has four good spades, he knows his partner has less than 11 points as he didn't bid at his first opportunity to bid so passing and converting the double to penalty is not a logical choice. Jumping in hearts to show a stronger hand is impractical as game is unlikely.

South bids hearts at the lowest level, 3♥.

Competitive Doubles

Board 9
North Deals
E-W Vul

	♠ A 4
	♥ K J 7
	♦ 4 3
	♣ A K J 10 7 3

	♠ Q J 9 7			♠ K 5 3
	♥ 10 4	N		♥ 8 5 3
	♦ K 10 2	W E		♦ A Q J 8 7 6
	♣ 9 8 5 2	S		♣ 4

	♠ 10 8 6 2
	♥ A Q 9 6 2
	♦ 9 5
	♣ Q 6

West	North	East	South
	1 ♣	1 ♦	1 ♥
Dbl	Rdbl	Pass	2 ♥
Pass	3 ♣	Pass	4 ♥
Pass	Pass	Pass	

West's double is a Snapdragon Double showing four spades and the values to respond.

North's Redouble is a Support Redouble showing three hearts.

South's 2♥ bid neither confirms nor denies the number of hearts he holds. It simply shows a minimum hand.

North's 3♣ bid shows long (6+) clubs and a medium hand (15-17) in strength.

South's 4♥ bid confirms five or more hearts and shows the values for game.

Competitive Doubles

Board 10
East Deals
Both Vul

		♠ A 2
		♥ Q 6 2
		♦ A K 9 8 5
		♣ J 5 3

♠ K 10 6 5 4 3		♠ J 8 7
♥ 7	N	♥ A K 10 8 5 4
♦ J 10 7 2	W E	♦ 3
♣ Q 4	S	♣ A 7 6

		♠ Q 9
		♥ J 9 3
		♦ Q 6 4
		♣ K 10 9 8 2

West	North	East	South
		1 ♥	Pass
1 ♠	2 ♦	Dbl	3 ♦
Pass	Pass	3 ♥	Pass
3 ♠	Pass	Pass	Pass

East's double is a Support Double.

East's double promises three card spade support.

West's pass does not deny nor confirm the number of spades he holds. It simply denies the desire to bid at the three level.

East competes to 3♥ showing 6+ hearts and a desire to compete.

West corrects to 3♠, confirming 5+ spades and a weak hand.

Competitive Doubles

Board 11
South Deals
None Vul

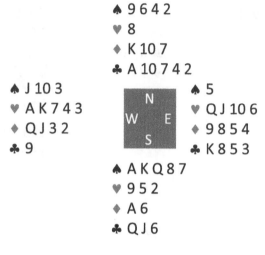

	♠ 9 6 4 2	
	♥ 8	
	♦ K 10 7	
	♣ A 10 7 4 2	

♠ J 10 3   ♠ 5
♥ A K 7 4 3   ♥ Q J 10 6
♦ Q J 3 2   ♦ 9 8 5 4
♣ 9   ♣ K 8 5 3

♠ A K Q 8 7
♥ 9 5 2
♦ A 6
♣ Q J 6

West	North	East	South
			1 ♠
2 ♥	2 ♠	3 ♥	Dbl
Pass	4 ♠	Pass	Pass
Pass			

South's double is a Maximal Double.

South shows a hand with the values for game if partner is at the top of his 2♠ bid.

North, with a singleton heart, four spades and the A♣ and K♦ feels that he has the values for game so bids 4♠.

Remember, without the values to invite game, South would have simply bid 3♠.

Competitive Doubles

Board 12
West Deals
N-S Vul

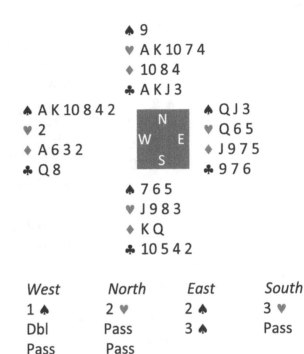

♠ 9
♥ A K 10 7 4
♦ 10 8 4
♣ A K J 3

♠ A K 10 8 4 2
♥ 2
♦ A 6 3 2
♣ Q 8

♠ Q J 3
♥ Q 6 5
♦ J 9 7 5
♣ 9 7 6

♠ 7 6 5
♥ J 9 8 3
♦ K Q
♣ 10 5 4 2

West	North	East	South
1 ♠	2 ♥	2 ♠	3 ♥
Dbl	Pass	3 ♠	Pass
Pass	Pass		

West's double is a Maximal Double.

West's double shows a hand with the values to invite game.

East bids 3♠ with a hand that does not have the values to play game.

Board 13
North Deals
Both Vul

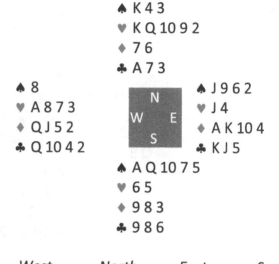

```
                        ♠ K 4 3
                        ♥ K Q 10 9 2
                        ♦ 7 6
                        ♣ A 7 3
        ♠ 8                         ♠ J 9 6 2
        ♥ A 8 7 3                   ♥ J 4
        ♦ Q J 5 2                   ♦ A K 10 4
        ♣ Q 10 4 2                  ♣ K J 5
                        ♠ A Q 10 7 5
                        ♥ 6 5
                        ♦ 9 8 3
                        ♣ 9 8 6
```

West	North	East	South
	1 ♥	Dbl	1 ♠
Dbl	1 N	2 ♦	Pass
Pass	Pass		

East's double is a Takeout Double.

East's double shows shortness in hearts, 11+ points and at least three cards in each of the remaining three suits.

West's double is a Responsive Double.

West's double shows both minor suits at least 4/4 and at least 6 points. East picks diamonds.

Competitive Doubles
Board 14
East Deals
None Vul

	♠ A 10 9 3	
	♥ 4	
	♦ Q 9 7 3	
	♣ K 6 5 4	

West		East
♠ Q J 7	N	♠ 6 5 2
♥ 7 6	W E	♥ A K Q 8 5 2
♦ J 6 4	S	♦ K 2
♣ A Q 9 8 3		♣ J 10

	♠ K 8 4	
	♥ J 10 9 3	
	♦ A 10 8 5	
	♣ 7 2	

West	North	East	South
		1 ♥	Pass
2 ♣	Pass	2 ♥	Pass
Pass	Dbl	Pass	3 ♦
Pass	Pass	Pass	

North's double is a Balancing Double.

North's double shows at least four diamonds and at least four spades. North's points are probably less than 11 (or he would have doubled at his first opportunity) but remember at his first opportunity, North was unsure how strong East/West's hands were. It was not until East showed a minimum hand by rebidding his suit at the minimum level and West showed a minimum hand by passing, that North felt confident that South had some values.

South chooses diamonds.

Competitive Doubles

Board 15
South Deals
N-S Vul

	♠ K Q 9 3 2		
	♥ Q 4 3		
	♦ J 9 5		
	♣ 9 3		

♠ 10 8 4		♠ 6
♥ K J		♥ 10 6 5 2
♦ K 10 7 4		♦ Q 8 3
♣ Q 8 6 4		♣ A K 7 5 2

	♠ A J 7 5		
	♥ A 9 8 7		
	♦ A 6 2		
	♣ J 10		

West	North	East	South
			1 ♦
Pass	1 ♠	Pass	2 ♠
Pass	Pass	Dbl	Pass
3 ♣	3 ♠	Pass	Pass
Pass			

East's double is a Balancing Double.

East's double promises at least four clubs and four hearts
and 8+ to 10 points.

West chooses clubs. Once North bids 3♠ East/West should
not bid again.

*Remember: once you have pushed the opponents one
level higher in the bidding. . .mission accomplished.
Don't bid again.*

Competitive Doubles

Board 16
West Deals
E-W Vul

```
                        ♠ 8 3
                        ♥ Q 4
                        ♦ A 8 6
                        ♣ K Q J 5 3 2
    ♠ A K J 6 5 2              ♠ 7
    ♥ K 3           N          ♥ A J 10 5
    ♦ K 3 2      W     E       ♦ Q J 9 5
    ♣ 9 8           S          ♣ A 10 7 4
                        ♠ Q 10 9 4
                        ♥ 9 8 7 6 2
                        ♦ 10 7 4
                        ♣ 6
```

West	North	East	South
1 ♠	2 ♣	Dbl	Pass
2 ♠	Pass	2 N	Pass
3 N	Pass	Pass	Pass

East's double is a Negative Double.

East's double is showing 6+ points and 4+ hearts. West rebids his spades and East now shows the value of his hand (11-12) by bidding 2NT.

Remember: East can not bid 2♥ at his turn to call because he has only four hearts and bidding 2♥ would promise at least five hearts.

Competitive Doubles

Board 17
North Deals
None Vul

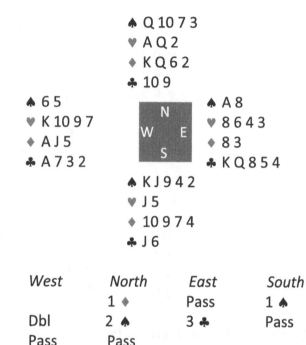

```
                        ♠ Q 10 7 3
                        ♥ A Q 2
                        ♦ K Q 6 2
                        ♣ 10 9
      ♠ 6 5                           ♠ A 8
      ♥ K 10 9 7          N           ♥ 8 6 4 3
      ♦ A J 5         W       E       ♦ 8 3
      ♣ A 7 3 2           S           ♣ K Q 8 5 4
                        ♠ K J 9 4 2
                        ♥ J 5
                        ♦ 10 9 7 4
                        ♣ J 6
```

West	North	East	South
	1 ♦	Pass	1 ♠
Dbl	2 ♠	3 ♣	Pass
Pass	Pass		

West's double is a Take-out Double.

Since two suits have been bid the double promises at least 4
cards in the two unbid suits and 11+ points.

Once North bids East does not have to bid, but chooses to
bid since he has a constructive hand (7-9 points or the
equivalent in distribution).

Competitive Doubles

Board 18
East Deals
E-W Vul

	♠ 10 6 4	
	♥ 10 8 6 2	
	♦ K 10 7 4	
	♣ J 6	

♠ K J 7 5		♠ A Q 8 2
♥ Q 9 4	N W E S	♥ 7
♦ 9 5		♦ J 8 6 3
♣ A K 5 4		♣ Q 9 7 2

	♠ 9 3	
	♥ A K J 5 3	
	♦ A Q 2	
	♣ 10 8 3	

West	North	East	South
		Pass	1 ♥
Pass	Pass	Dbl	Pass
2 ♠	Pass	Pass	Pass

East's double is a Balancing Double.

If East doesn't bid, the auction is over and the opponents will play 1♥.

East can double with fewer than 10 points since he has perfect shape (4-4-4-1) and is a passed hand.

West jumps to 2♠ to show a better hand (12+ to 14). West must have a better hand than the 9-12 points he would have promised when responding to a Take-out Double, as his partner did not have an opening hand.

East passes with sub-minimum values.

Competitive Doubles

Board 19
South Deals
None Vul

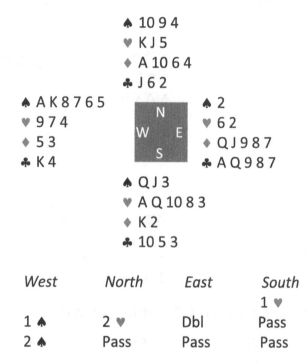

	♠ 10 9 4		
	♥ K J 5		
	♦ A 10 6 4		
	♣ J 6 2		

West	North	East	South
			1 ♥
1 ♠	2 ♥	Dbl	Pass
2 ♠	Pass	Pass	Pass

East's double is a Responsive Double.

East shows 4+ cards in each of the minor suits.

West shows long spades and no fit for either minor.

Competitive Doubles

Board 20
West Deals
E-W Vul

```
                    ♠ 8 3
                    ♥ Q 4
                    ♦ A 8 6
                    ♣ K Q J 5 3 2
   ♠ A K J 6 5 2                    ♠ 7
   ♥ K 3              N             ♥ A J 10 5
   ♦ K 3 2        W       E         ♦ Q J 9 5
   ♣ 9 8              S             ♣ A 10 7 4
                    ♠ Q 10 9 4
                    ♥ 9 8 7 6 2
                    ♦ 10 7 4
                    ♣ 6
```

West	North	East	South
1 ♠	2 ♣	Dbl	Pass
2 ♠	Pass	2 N	Pass
3 N	Pass	Pass	Pass

East's double is a Negative Double.

East's double is showing 6+ points and 4+ hearts. West rebids his spades and East now shows the value of his hand (11-12) by bidding 2NT.

Remember: East can not bid 2♥ at his turn to call because he has only four hearts and bidding 2♥ would promise at least five hearts.

Competitive Doubles

Board 21
North Deals
None Vul

```
                              ♠ K Q J 3 2
                              ♥ A Q
                              ♦ 7 3
                              ♣ 10 9 8 3
         ♠ 10 8 5                           ♠ 9 7 6
         ♥ J 10 6 3 2          N            ♥ K 9 8 7
         ♦ A 8 5           W       E        ♦ 6
         ♣ K 7                 S            ♣ A Q J 6 2
                              ♠ A 4
                              ♥ 5 4
                              ♦ K Q J 10 9 4 2
                              ♣ 5 4
```

West	North	East	South
	1 ♠	2 ♣	2 ♦
Dbl	Pass	2 ♥	Pass
Pass	Pass		

West's double is Snapdragon.

West's double shows 6+ points and 5+ hearts. With a fit in hearts but minimum values, East simply bids 2♥.

Board 22
East Deals
Both Vul

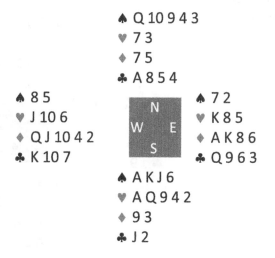

	♠ Q 10 9 4 3	
	♥ 7 3	
	♦ 7 5	
	♣ A 8 5 4	

♠ 8 5		♠ 7 2
♥ J 10 6		♥ K 8 5
♦ Q J 10 4 2		♦ A K 8 6
♣ K 10 7		♣ Q 9 6 3

	♠ A K J 6	
	♥ A Q 9 4 2	
	♦ 9 3	
	♣ J 2	

West	North	East	South
		1 ♦	1 ♥
2 ♦	Dbl	Pass	2 ♠
Pass	Pass	Pass	

North's double is a Responsive Double.

North's double shows at least four cards in spades and clubs and at least 6 points.

South picks spades.

Board 23
South Deals
E-W Vul

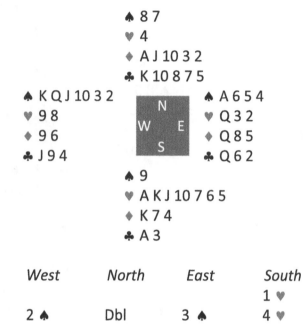

	West	North	East	South
				1 ♥
	2 ♠	Dbl	3 ♠	4 ♥
	Pass	Pass	Pass	

North's double is a Negative Double.

Since both majors have been bid this double is promising both minors. It also shows some values as he would be forcing his partner to choose a minor at the three level.

South's 4♥ bid shows a self-sufficient suit and a hand that he believes will make game opposite partner's Negative Double.

Competitive Doubles

Board 24
West Deals
N-S Vul

```
                    ♠ A K J 7 6 4 2
                    ♥ 3
                    ♦ J 5
                    ♣ 7 5 4
        ♠ 10                          ♠ Q 9 8 5
        ♥ A K Q 7 4        N          ♥ 10 2
        ♦ A Q 6 4      W       E      ♦ 8 7 2
        ♣ K 9 8            S          ♣ A J 6 3
                    ♠ 3
                    ♥ J 9 8 6 5
                    ♦ K 10 9 3
                    ♣ Q 10 2
```

West	North	East	South
1 ♥	3 ♠	Pass	Pass
Dbl	Pass	Pass	Pass

West's double is a Re-opening Double.

East passes West's double to convert the take-out double to
a penalty double. East expects that West will have a strong
hand (15+) since his double would force East to bid at the
four-level. East has two definite tricks, one spade and one
club, and expects that he could have another with his fourth
spade.

***Remember that if East had doubled at his first opportunity
to bid, his double would have been a Negative Double.***

The
'Winning Bridge Conventions'
Series

Competitive Doubles
Conventions after a Notrump Opening
Conventions after a Major Suit Opening
Competitive Bidding
Conventions Useful with Strong Hands
Conventions Useful with 2/1
Slam Bidding Conventions
Defensive Carding & Opening Leads

Master Point Press
416-781-0351
www.masterpointpress.com
Email: info@masterpointpress.com